GAMES FOR
NAUGHTY PEOPLE

BY BRIAN L. PELLHAM

Edited by Sally Neary
Front Cover Art by Robert Brunz
Cover Design by Scott Ware
Artwork by Aron Ahlstrom, Scott Holland, and Karen Sarafin
Photography by David Baack

Special thanks to Kim Adams, Brian Bannister, David Bates,
Daniel Bendzak, Matt Calkins, Beth Chmielowski, Shane
Cooley, Diane Cothren, Marybeth Cothren, Chris Ecklund,
Mark Gustafson, May Gustafson, Eric Hutcheson, John Kaye,
Allison Kent, Gary Kretzchmar, Maria Jurado, Jason Hintze,
Will Halpern, Steve Johnson, Clint Kendrick, David Laing,
Winston Lin, Clara Pellham, Tony Pellham, Jeff Rodgers,
Emily Ross, RPlace, Erich Schneider, Vinita Sidhu, Steve
Sindiong, Adam Stroh, Matt Strong, Chad Tibbits, Terrence
Tung, and Danny Wallace for their contributions.

Inquiries should be addressed to
Kheper Publishing
P.O. Box 906
Bellevue, WA 98112
kheperpublishing@yahoo.com

Printed and bound in the United States of America.

DEDICATED TO THE
NAUGHTIEST OF THEM ALL,
MY CAT BUBASTIS

Other books by Brian L. Pellham:

- A Partier's Guide to 51 Drinking Games
- Outrageous Party Games (Coauthored by Allison Kent)
- Egyptian Hieroglyphics and Their Meanings

ABOUT THE AUTHOR

Brian L. Pellham is a whore and a drunk. He is also wanted in nine states for crimes that he has committed against man, nature, and portable restrooms. When he is not in prison or rehab, he spends most of his time cruising the nightclubs.

When questioned by the police, his neighbors usually describe Brian as a quiet man who keeps to himself. His favorite color is blood red, he loves gerbils, and he enjoys belching in public. His hobbies include calling 1-900 numbers, submitting articles to the tabloids, and running with scissors. Also, he has only two months to live, because he did not begin treatment for his syphilis early enough.

Okay......seriously, Brian L. Pellham is just an average Joe who enjoys being naughty once in a while.

TABLE OF CONTENTS

Dear Readers,

Thank you for your interest in *Games for Naughty People*. This is my third games book, and I expect there will be many more to come. I decided to write a book on naughty games because I think it's very important for adults of all ages to learn to embrace times when they have been "bad." Equally important is learning how to be naughty in nice ways. My goal with this book is to offer numerous games that allow you to explore your mischievousness in a campy and socially acceptable way.

As children, most of us were punished when we were naughty. As time went on, we learned to repress our desires to act out our deviant impulses. This helped us to fit into society as we matured, but it also sticks us with the idea that we are still being "bad," even when it's socially acceptable and appropriate for us to be naughty.

It's often difficult to determine when it is appropriate to be naughty. One of the most acceptable times to channel your occasional need to be "bad" is while you are making love. In fact, many sex therapists recommend being naughty with your partner as a healthy way to keep your relationship alive.

I agree that it's important to be naughty with your partner. I also feel that it's important for us to be naughty in other parts of our lives (especially for those of us who are single). That is why I invite you to experience the many ways that *Games for Naughty People* allows you to explore being naughty.

All of the games in *Games for Naughty People* are original ideas that you will not find in print elsewhere. All games have been thoroughly tested and I guarantee that there are games in here that even your most conservative friends can enjoy.

To assist you in selecting the most appropriate games, I organized the chapters by the category of naughty behavior. Also, symbols at the beginning of each game serve as a handy reference to let you know what type of game you are considering. (Symbol definitions appear on page 11.)

You are welcome to contact me if you have an original game idea. I might be interested in using your game in a future publication. You can contact me through Kheper Publishing (see page 2 for the address).

I hope you enjoy playing the games in my book.

Sincerely,
Brian Pellham

SYMBOLS

 = Recommended as an icebreaker for large groups.

 = A prize should be offered to the winner.

 = Works better with an audience of people who are not actual players of the game.

 = Requires an outgoing member of the group to volunteer as the emcee.

 = There is a secret to this game. The rules should not be shared with the entire group.

 = May be best if this game is played outdoors.

 = Best for players who know each other well.

 = You may wish (or need) to make photocopies while setting up for this game.

 = One or more players may be required to get buck naked at some point during this game.

WARNING!

If you have deep, dark secrets, you may not want to play the GOSSIP games. You should also consider what secrets about your friends you can share, and which ones you cannot, before playing these games.

GOSSIP

BIG MOUTH

Number of Players 4+

Supplies

- A hat (or similar container)
- A sheet of paper (for keeping score)
- One strip of paper per player
- Several pens or pencils

Setup

One of the players, typically the host of the party, emcees the game. Each player (including the emcee) thinks of a piece of naughty gossip about any of the other players and writes it down on a strip of paper. The gossip can also be about the emcee or other party guests who are not participating in the game. A gossip statement should not include the name of the person that the gossip is about. Instead, each player should write the name of the person that the gossip is about after the gossip statement and in parentheses. An example of a suitable entry is "Last weekend, this person got drunk at a restaurant and hooked up with the maitre d'. (Matt)". The completed entry should be folded and placed in the hat. After everyone has submitted their entries, the emcee takes the hat and sits at the front of the room.

Play

The emcee draws an entry out of the hat and reads the gossip statement to the group, but does not read the name that follows the gossip statement. If a player thinks he knows the answer, he should yell it out. He is allowed to guess only once. If he is incorrect, the emcee informs him that he has not guessed the answer and waits for another player to wager a guess. When someone guesses correctly, the emcee writes down a point for her and then discards the entry. Next, the emcee presents a second entry and continues presenting the entries until they all have been guessed.

Players should be encouraged to place guesses even if they are unsure as to whom the gossip is about. If all players are disqualified from wagering guesses before a secret is uncovered, the emcee should discard the entry without revealing whom the gossip is about.

Ending the Game

The game ends after the emcee has presented all of the entries. The player with the highest number of correct guesses wins the game. If there is a tie, the emcee should break the tie by offering a piece of gossip that she knows about one of the other players. Only the players caught in the tie are allowed to guess. They take turns wagering guesses until one of them stumbles on the correct player and thereby wins the game. A prize should be presented to the winner.

WHO HAVE YOU DONE?

Number of Players 5+

Supplies
- A stopwatch (or clock)
- One list per player
- One pen or pencil per player

Setup

The host makes copies of the Who Have You Done List that follows this game (if the party guests have slept around a lot, she should instead distribute the Whores Version that follows the first list). She should make enough copies to provide each participant with his or her own list.

The host distributes copies immediately before play begins. She does not collect signatures or sign lists. She collects the completed lists, performs accuracy checks, and addresses any questions that arise.

Play

The group has ten minutes to get to know one another better by discovering who in the room has engaged in sexual relations with the types of people described on the list. Once the host starts the stopwatch, players begin mingling. Players can only sign other people's names to the lists; they cannot sign their own names. Players also cannot answer questions about themselves but they can answer questions about other players. Honesty is very important; players should only sign names for other people if they believe they are accurate in doing so.

For groups of ten or more, players should be permitted to have each person's name only once on their pages. If the group is not large enough for this rule, players may have names written on their lists more than once, but they cannot have the same name appear more than three times.

Ending the Game

The participant who collects signatures for all descriptions on the list first (within the allotted ten minutes) submits her list to the host. The host then reviews the list to make sure that it is complete and accurate. The host tells the players to stop what they are doing, then calls out the names on the list in order to verify the signatures with the group. After the host calls out a name, that player should say whether or not he has had sexual relations with someone that fits the description. If he has, the host continues through the list. If he hasn't, the host crosses off the name, returns the card to the player, and the game continues.

If players cannot complete their lists (i.e., if there are one or more descriptions to which no one confesses), the person who submits the most complete and accurate list after ten minutes wins the game. A prize should be offered to encourage players to socialize more and complete their lists.

WHO HAVE YOU DONE LIST

Locate other players who have had sexual relations with the following types of people:

Someone who is 7+ years older _____

Someone who is 7+ years younger _____

A teacher or instructor _____

Someone who is under the age of 18 _____

The best friend of a current or ex-lover _____

Someone who was picked up at a bar _____

Two other people at the same time _____

A prostitute _____

A family friend _____

A woman who was currently menstruating _____

WHO HAVE YOU DONE LIST – Whores Version

Locate other players who have had sexual relations with the following types of people:

A homeless person _____

A relative (distant cousins count) _____

Someone with an STD _____

A famous person _____

A transvestite _____

Two strangers (separately) in one evening _____

Two strangers at the same time _____

Someone who just got out of prison _____

Someone who was high on drugs _____

A married couple _____

SPREAD THE WORD

Number of Players 4+

Supplies
- A sheet of poster board
- Four tacks (or heavy-duty tape)
- A felt-tip marker

Setup
Before the party, the host informs her expected guests that three false rumors will be spread at her party. The rumors will be about guests who are attending, and will not start from her directly. She thinks up three false rumors and then calls three friends to enlist their aid in spreading the rumors at the party.

Play
The assistants begin by telling the false rumors at the party. The host should not tell any of the false rumors and the assistants should not let people know that they are helping with the game. After telling someone a rumor, the rumor-spreader should tell the recipient that he must not let anyone know who told him the rumor. Later in the evening, the recipient should share the rumor with another party guest, and he too should ask that the recipient not tell anyone who told her the rumor.

The host, assistants, and other party guests should also be encouraged to share secrets that they know about other people

20

at the party. These secrets should be things that the guests have honestly heard about other guests.

At the end of the night (before guests begin leaving), the host tacks up the poster board and asks everyone to sit around it. She then asks people to share the rumors that they have heard throughout the party. As guests share rumors, she writes them on the board. The assistants should eventually share the false rumors, if no one else shares them, with the appropriate details.

After the host has posted a set of rumors, she then asks the group to vote on which rumors they think are false. Players should only raise their hands three times, once for each rumor they think is false. The host tallies the votes by counting the number of people who raise their hands as she points to each particular rumor. She should write the totals on the board. The assistants are allowed to vote for the false rumors, but still should not reveal their roles in the game. After all rumors have been voted on, the host reveals the three false rumors.

Ending the Game
The winner(s) of the game is the subject of the "true" rumor that receives the most votes. As winner(s), the player(s) should be allowed the first opportunity to deny the rumor to the rest of the group.

WARNING!

Be careful what you confess to while playing CRIMINAL ACTIVITY games. You should not play these games if you are on trial for a crime that you actually did commit, especially if other players may be called to the witness stand. Also, it is recommended that you do not play these games with your parole officer.

CRIMINAL

ACTIVITY

WHO DID IT?

Number of Players 6+

Supplies
- A hat (or similar container)
- A piece of paper (for keeping score)
- Two large strips of paper per player
- Several pens or pencils

Setup

Each player writes down two crimes that he or she has committed, followed by his or her name in parentheses. The two entries should be written down separately on the strips of paper provided. The crimes can be any actions that are against the law. The group should be encouraged to be creative and descriptive with the crimes they submit for the game. If the puritans of the group have difficulty coming up with crimes, they should be reminded that even jaywalking and drinking at age twelve are violations of the law.

Each player should fold his or her entries in half, then write the names of any two players on the outside of each entry. A player may write his own name on the outside of his entry. If others in the room are familiar with a crime that he has committed, he may wish to include them in the two names that are written on the outside of the entry. Completed entries should be placed in the hat.

Play

One of the players draws an entry from the hat. She calls out the two names that are written on it, but does not read the crime description. The two players that are named take the entry and silently read the crime. They can take a minute or two to review and discuss the crime, then they act it out for the other players. The players are allowed to act or say almost anything while reenacting the crime. The only thing they are not allowed to do is speak names, including names of the people that the crimes have been committed against.

Throughout the skit, players wager guesses as to who has committed the crime. Each player is only allowed one guess and the person who actually committed the crime cannot guess herself. The actors continue acting until someone guesses the correct author, or their skit reaches a natural ending point. If the actors finish the skit before the author is guessed, they should prompt the crowd to continue guessing.

If a player guesses correctly, he receives one point. If no one guesses correctly, the actors reveal the name of the player who committed the crime and the entry is discarded. The player who guesses correctly (or a volunteer if no one guesses correctly) draws the next entry from the hat and initiates the next round.

Ending the Game

Play continues until all entries have been acted out. The player(s) with the most points at the end of the game is the winner. The host should award a prize to the winner(s).

FALSE ACCUSATIONS

Number of Players 5+

Setup
Players sit in a circle.

Play
Player One begins by making a false accusation about one of the other players. A false accusation must pertain to a criminal activity. An example of an appropriate false accusation is "John stalked the used car salesman." The subject of Player One's false accusation must then come up with a false accusation about another player. The false accusation cannot be a repeat of a previous player's false accusation. Players can make false accusations about any of the players, including themselves.

A player must exit the game if he makes any one of the following mistakes:

- Repeating a false accusation. What matters with this rule is the verb. If one player uses "stab" in his false accusation, other players cannot use the same verb later.
- Using synonyms of verbs in a false accusation. If one player uses "beat up" in her false accusation, other players cannot use similar verbs later (e.g., punched, hit, or clobbered).

- Making a false accusation that is not a criminal activity. For example, "Allison left the seat up" is not an action that could have her imprisoned or fined.
- Making a false accusation out of turn. For example, if Player One is the subject of the first false accusation and Player Two starts to make the next false accusation, Player Two must exit the game.
- Making an accusation about someone who is not a current participant of the game.
- Making an accusation about another player that is true.

Players continue making false accusations about each other and gradually eliminate participants from the game.

Ending the Game

The last player remaining in the game is considered the winner. The host should award him a prize.

WARNING!

If you have a weak stomach you may not want to participate in the VULGARITY games. Also, the scavenger hunt and scavenger bingo games require that you take photographs of some really disgusting things. No matter how great the temptation, you should refrain from handling items, such as roadkill. Staying several feet away from the items you photograph will keep you out of reach of the germs they carry.

VULGARITY

THAT'S DISGUSTING!

Number of Players 8

Supplies
- Four chairs
- A stopwatch (or clock)
- A hat (or similar container)
- A piece of paper (for keeping score)
- Eight strips of paper
- A pen or pencil

Setup
There are eight topics for this game:

- Bathroom mishaps
- Sexual endeavors
- Insects and vermin
- Vomit
- Trash
- Snot
- Blood and guts
- Rotting things

One of the players, typically the host of the party, emcees the game. He writes down the eight topics individually on strips of paper. He folds them and places them in a hat. The emcee

then places four chairs at the front of the room and asks for
four volunteers. He selects the volunteers and they seat
themselves in the chairs at the front of the room.

Play

The emcee begins the first round by selecting one of the topics
and presenting it to the first contestant. The first contestant has
two minutes to think of the most disgusting story she can tell
(that pertains to the topic presented). After the two minute
preparation time elapses, the first contestant tells her story.
The story must be true and she must be a main character in it.
She has only two minutes to tell her story and should attempt
to disgust the crowd as much as possible. The emcee should
cut the player off if her story exceeds two minutes.

Next, the emcee selects a second topic and the second
contestant has two minutes to prepare and then two minutes to
tell his most disgusting true story (that pertains to the topic
presented). Then, a third topic is drawn and the third
contestant prepares and shares a disgusting true story. Finally,
the fourth contestant draws a topic and tells a story.

After all players have shared their stories on the topic, the
emcee asks the audience to vote on the story that they found
the most disgusting. The emcee names the contestants one by
one and the members of the audience raise their hands after the
name of their selected winner is called. If there is a tie, the
audience breaks the tie by voting on who they believe the
winner should be. (Only the contestants who are part of the tie
should be included in the vote.)

In the second round, new contestants challenge the winner of the first round. The three runners-up return to the audience as the emcee selects three new volunteers to take their seats. The returning champion is the first storyteller for the second round. The emcee draws a topic and the contestant prepares and shares a two minute story. The emcee determines which contestants tell the next two stories, and the remaining contestant tells the final story. The audience again votes for the contestant who has shared the most disgusting tale.

Ending the Game

If the returning champion wins the second round, he also becomes the winner of the game. If another player wins the second round, both she and the returning champion are winners of the game.

PHOTO SCAVENGER HUNT

Number of Players 6+

Supplies
- One stopwatch (or wristwatch) per team
- One camera (preferably an instant one) per team

Setup
The host creates a list of disgusting actions and items for her guests to capture on film. A sample list follows this game. The host divides the participants into even teams and provides them with identical lists. The host assigns a time limit to the game and tells players where they need to meet after they complete their lists or before their time expires. Each team should have only one camera available for their use. Because the items on the list are disgusting, the teams should be discouraged from handling them directly.

Play
Players review their lists and accompany their teammates as each team attempts to photograph as many items on the list as possible in the allotted time frame. Each team should return to where the host is waiting after they complete their lists. If a team's list is not yet complete, the team members should still return to the host before the time limit is over. Any teams that are late are disqualified.

Ending the Game

After all teams have returned, or as soon as the time expires, the host reviews the photographs of the qualifying teams. (If teams did not use instant cameras, the host will first need to develop the film at a one hour photo shop.) The host decides whether or not the photographs accurately depict the items on the list. Whichever team has photographed the most items in the allotted time wins the game. If several teams have completed their lists, the team that had presented photos (or film) to the host first is the winner. Since this is a very challenging game, the host should reward prizes to all members of the winning team.

Variation

The host could award the prizes to the team that has the most disgusting collection of photographs. Photographing the most items or finishing first do not matter in this variation. The judge decides which team's collection is the most digusting. Teams should still arrive before the time limit ends to qualify for the competition.

SAMPLE PHOTO SCAVENGER HUNT LIST

You have four hours to photograph the actions and items on this list.

(Do not handle any of these items.)

1. Roadkill.
2. A clogged toilet.
3. A man (not a team member) using a urinal.
4. Photos of three different types of animal feces.
5. A cat using a litter box.
6. A used tampon or pad.
7. A city dump.
8. All of the team members watching a porno that stars obese people. (Someone who is not on the team must take the photograph.)
9. A person (not a team member) in lingerie.
10. A slug or snail, and its trail.

PHOTO SCAVENGER BINGO

Number of Players 6+

Supplies
- One camera (preferably an instant one) per team

Setup

The host creates several bingo cards that list disgusting actions and items for her guests to capture on film. The various bingo cards can contain similar entries, but they should be organized differently. (Sample bingo cards follow this game.)

The host divides the participants into even teams and provides each team with one scavenger bingo card. Each team should have only one camera available for their use. Because the items on the cards are disgusting, all players must be discouraged from handling them directly.

Play

Players review their cards and accompany their teammates as each team attempts to photograph specific items on their cards to score a scavenger bingo. A scavenger bingo can be five items that are aligned horizontally, vertically, or diagonally. Once a team achieves a scavenger bingo, the team members should return to where the host is waiting.

Ending the Game

After all teams have returned, the host reviews the photographs of the team that returned first. (If teams did not use instant cameras, the host will first need to develop the film at a one hour photo shop.) The host decides whether or not the photographs accurately depict the items that make up the scavenger bingo. If the team achieves a satisfactory scavenger bingo, they win the game. If they do not achieve a satisfactory scavenger bingo, the host reviews the photos of the second team. All members of the team that returned to the host first (with a satisfactory scavenger bingo) should be awarded prizes.

SAMPLE SCAVENGER BINGO CARDS

SCAVENGER BINGO CARD ONE
(Do not handle any of these items.)

VOMIT	FULL DUMPSTER	DEAD OPOSSUM	SLUG	ROTTEN APPLE
DOG PEEING	CITY DUMP	CLOGGED TOILET	SNAIL	POLLUTED AIR
USED TAMPON	ROTTEN TOOTH	**** FREE SPACE ****	CROTCH-LESS PANTIES	THROWN-UP HAIRBALL
ADULT VIDEO STORE	COW PIE	TABLE IN BUTCHER SHOP	SWAMP	STAINED DENTURES
HORSE CRAP	DIRTY BARBEQUE	BATHROOM WALL GRAFFITI	DIRTY ASHTRAY	USED DIAPER

SCAVENGER BINGO CARD TWO

(Do not handle any of these items.)

ROTTEN BANANAS	MAGGOTS	DIARRHEA	FRESHLY POPPED ZIT	MOLDY BREAD
DIRTY LITTER BOX	COCK-ROACH	RAT	RABBIT POOP	TATTOOED BUTTOCK
UNDER-WEAR STREAK MARKS	PIERCED NIPPLE	**** FREE SPACE ****	ANIMALS MATING	ANT HILL
MAN WITH EGG ON FACE	FULL DRYER LINT TRAP	STATUE COVERED IN BIRD CRAP	PILE OF CUT HAIR	SPOILED MILK LUMPS
CITY DUMP	FAKE DOG POOP	COW PIE	DIRTY ASHTRAY	USED TAMPON

SCAVENGER BINGO CARD THREE

(Do not handle any of these items.)

OUT-HOUSE	MOLDY BREAD	UNDER-WEAR STREAK MARKS	ANT HILL	STATUE COVERED IN BIRD CRAP
PILE OF CUT HAIR	SPOILED MILK LUMPS	FAKE DOG POOP	VOMIT	FULL DUMPSTER
DOG PEEING	SNAIL	**** FREE SPACE ****	HORSE CRAP	ROTTEN TOOTH
STAINED DENTURES	BATHROOM WALL GRAFFITI	USED TAMPON	ADULT VIDEO STORE	THROWN-UP HAIRBALL
COCK-ROACH	ROTTEN TOMATO	ENEMA BAG	SLUG	FRESHLY POPPED ZIT

SCAVENGER BINGO CARD FOUR

(Do not handle any of these items.)

DAN-DRUFF	MAGGOTS	MOLDY BREAD	OUT-HOUSE	BACON GREASE
BEN-WA BALLS	DEAD OPOSSUM	FULL DUMPSTER	DOG PEEING	CLOGGED TOILET
MAN WITH EGG ON FACE	STATUE COVERED IN BIRD CRAP	**** FREE SPACE ****	PILE OF CUT HAIR	RABBIT POOP
TABLE IN BUTCHER SHOP	STAINED CARPET	POLLUTED AIR	SWAMP	DIRTY BARBEQUE
CROTCH-LESS PANTIES	DIRTY ASHTRAY	ANT HILL	SPOILED MILK LUMP	FULL LITTER BOX

WARNING!

If you are sensitive about your loose morals, you may not want to play DIRTY TALK games. However, if you are comfortable with yourself, these games do present great opportunities for you to discover what your friends really think of you.

DIRTY

TALK

WHAT'S YOUR PRICE?

Number of Players 4+

Supplies
- A piece of paper (for keeping score)
- Ten strips of paper per player
- One pen or pencil per player

Setup
One of the players, typically the host of the party, emcees the
game. In preparation for this game, he needs to develop a list
of ten questions. (A sample list follows this game.) Each
question should ask how much a guest would need to be paid
to perform a certain unpleasant act. An example is "How
much would I have to pay you to glue your lips together?" The
questions should be actions that the audience members could
actually be paid to carry out. An example of a bad question is
"How much would I have to pay you to stab yourself in the
chest with an ice pick?"

The emcee places three chairs at the front of the room and asks
for three volunteers. He selects the players and they seat
themselves in the chairs at the front of the room.

Play
The host begins the game by asking one of the audience
members the first question from his list. The audience member

then considers how much it would take to get her to perform the unpleasant act that was presented to her. At the same time, the three players are attempting to guess how much it would take for the particular audience member to perform the action. Anyone can ask the emcee to elaborate on the question during this time. Consider the previous example question "How much would I have to pay you to glue your lips together?" A player may want to ask what type of glue would be used. Players can adjust their answers accordingly after the emcee addresses any questions.

Once all three players have written down dollar amounts, the answers are locked in and no more questions can be asked. The audience member announces her answer. Then the players reveal their answers. The player who guesses the closest, without going over, scores a point. For example, if the audience member says $5,000, Player One guesses $10,000, Player Two guesses $3,000, and Player Three guesses $5,500, Player Two scores the point because Player One and Player Three both overbid. If all three players overbid, no one receives a point and the question is discarded. The emcee then poses a second question to one of the audience members.

Ending the Game
The emcee continues asking questions of various audience members until all ten questions have been answered. At this point, the emcee tallies the score and awards the prize to the player with the highest score. If there is a tie, the emcee should come up with a tie-breaking question. The person that scores the final point breaks the tie and wins the prize.

SAMPLE WHAT'S YOUR PRICE QUESTIONS

1. How much would I have to pay you to swallow a dozen raw eggs?
2. How much would I have to pay you to completely burn up all of your possessions?
3. How much would I have to pay you to sleep with Player Two?
4. How much would I have to pay you to shave off all of your body hair?
5. How much would I have to pay you to masturbate in front of everyone in this room?
6. How much would I have to pay you to call your boss right now and tell her you quit your job?
7. How much would I have to pay you to give Player One an enema?
8. How much would I have to pay you to show up at your favorite dance club wearing only a diaper?
9. How much would I have to pay you to change the oil in Player Three's car?
10. How much would I have to pay you to squirt a container of mustard into your underpants?

MOST LIKELY

Number of Players 3+

Setup

Players sit in a circle.

Play

Player One begins by asking a Most Likely Question. Most Likely Questions are posed to the entire group and should ask who the players think is most likely to carry out an action or behave a certain way. Sample questions include "Which player is most likely to rob a bank?" and "Who has the worst table manners?" A list of additional sample Most Likely Questions follows this game.

After asking the first question, Player One then gives the group a minute or two to think of their answers. Then, starting to the left of Player One, the other players announce their answers. Players can only name other players' names when answering the question. Any player in the circle is eligible (i.e., a player can name himself as well as any other player). The person who asked the question (Player One) keeps track of the answers and informs the group as to who has won the most votes. The person who wins comes up with the next question. If two or more players tie, Player One breaks the tie by selecting one of these players to ask the next question.

Ending the Game

Play continues until the game has reached a natural ending point. There are no winners to this game.

SAMPLE MOST LIKELY QUESTIONS

1. Which player has slept around the most?
2. Who is the biggest gossip?
3. Which player is most likely to develop hemorrhoids?
4. Who is most likely to be arrested for indecent exposure?
5. Who would make the best housewife (or househusband)?
6. Which player has the poorest hygiene?
7. Who do you suppose looks the best with their clothes off?
8. Which player would survive the longest if everyone were stranded on a deserted island?
9. Who is most likely to fall asleep while making love?
10. Which player has the most annoying habits?
11. Who do you think was teased the most in high school?
12. Who do you suspect has the most body hair?
13. Who do you think was the pudgiest baby?
14. Which player is most likely to end up homeless?
15. Which player do you suspect uses the most toilet paper in a given week?
16. Who do you suppose has the naughtiest dreams?
17. Which player is most likely to switch careers in the next couple months?
18. Which player do you suspect is the most inhibited while making love?
19. Which player would make the best gubernatorial candidate?
20. Who is likely to complain the most if the group was forced to play this game for another three hours?

PREDICTIONS

Number of Players 6 (3 couples)

Supplies
- One chair per player
- One sheet of paper (for keeping score)
- Six pieces of white cardboard (or large index cards) per couple
- One marker per couple

Setup

One of the players, typically the host of the party, emcees the game. In preparation for this game, he needs to develop a list of six statements containing one or two blanks. The emcee should base the statements on the couples' relationships, likes and dislikes, and/or love making techniques. Statements with multiple choice answers and two part statements are allowed. An example of an appropriate two part statement is "In bed, my partner is better at ___(blank)___; I am better at ___(blank)___." A list of additional sample statements follows this game.

The host sets up six chairs at the front of the room. They should face the audience and should be grouped into three sets of two.

Play

The emcee begins the game by asking for three couples to volunteer. The couples take the seats at the front of the room. Each volunteering couple needs to assign roles to themselves; one is the husband and the other is the wife (this step is especially important for same-sex couples).

The emcee asks the wives to leave the room and leads them to a location secluded enough from the game so that they cannot hear the voices of their husbands or the audience. The emcee then returns to the game and asks the first question of Husband One. Husband One answers the question and writes his answer down on one of his pieces of cardboard. Next Husband Two answers the question and writes down his answer, then Husband Three does the same.

The second question is posed to Husband Two first, then to Husband Three, followed by Husband One. The third question is posed first to Husband Three, then to Husband One, followed by Husband Two. At this point, the husbands should have three cards with their answers written on them. They should place them face down in their laps, with the first answer on top and the third at the bottom of the stack.

The emcee retrieves the wives, and they return to their seats next to their husbands. The emcee asks the first question to Wife One. Wife One wagers an answer, then Husband One holds up the card with his answer. If their answers are similar, the couple scores one point. If there is uncertainty as to whether or not the answers are similar, the emcee makes the judgment call. Next the emcee poses the first question to Wife Two, then to Wife Three. The second question is posed first to Wife Two, and the third question is posed first to Wife Three.

At the end of the round, the emcee tallies the points and announces the score. Now it is the husbands' turn to leave the room. The emcee escorts them out, then asks three new questions to the wives. The order in which he asks the questions is the same as he did with the husbands. After all three wives answer three questions the emcee summons the husbands. The husbands then attempt to match their wives answers in the same manner as the wives did in the first round.

Ending the Game

The game ends after round two is completed. The couple with the most points wins the game. If there is a tie, the audience should vote for the couple that gave the most entertaining answers. The couple receiving the most votes is deemed the winner. The emcee should award prizes to the winning couple.

SAMPLE PREDICTION STATEMENTS

(To be posed first to the husbands.)

1. My wife's most annoying habit is _____.
2. In a past life, my wife was most likely _____.
   a) Joan of Arc
   b) Lady Godiva
   c) Emily Dickinson
3. If all of the world's _____ were destroyed, my wife would probably have a nervous breakdown.
   a) telephones
   b) department stores
   c) chocolate factories
4. My wife is most likely to win a _____ contest.
   a) wet t-shirt
   b) log-rolling
   c) bake-off
5. In high school, my wife should have been voted most likely to _____.
6. When I come home from work, I am most likely to catch my wife _____.
   a) gossiping with her friends
   b) flipping through mail-order catalogs
   c) watching soap operas

SAMPLE PREDICTION STATEMENTS

(To be posed first to the wives.)

1. The career that my husband is least suited for is

    _____.

    a) handyman
    b) guidance counselor
    c) porno star

2. My husband sometimes struts around as if his _____
    was bigger than it actually is.

    a) paycheck
    b) brain
    c) penis

3. I am most embarrassed when my husband _____ in
    public.

4. My husband's most recent ex-girlfriend resembles

    _____.

    a) me
    b) his mother
    c) a tree sloth

5. My husband's idea of a romantic evening is _____.

    a) bringing roses and having a candlelight dinner
    b) buying a six-pack and renting a porno
    c) doing the dishes and giving a backrub

6. The most sexually outlandish thing that my husband has
    suggested is _____.

WARNING!

The COUPLES ONLY games involve physical contact between two players. Play these games with your current lover or someone with whom you wish to be intimate. Be sure to practice safe sex and use protection when the games call for sexual contact.

COUPLES

ONLY

FOREPLAY

Number of Couples 1

Supplies
• Two six-sided dice (varying in size and/or color)

Setup
The couple assigns verbs to the six numbers of the first die. The verbs should be actions that players would like to perform on each other. Examples of six actions are (1) kiss, (2) lick, (3) caress, (4) suck, (5) nibble, and (6) stroke. The couple then assigns body parts to the six numbers of the second die. Examples of six body parts are (1) lips, (2) ear, (3) neck, (4) chest, (5) navel, and (6) genitalia.

Play
Player One rolls the dice and performs the action from the first die on the body part of Player Two that is specified by the second die. Then Player Two rolls the dice and performs the appropriate action on Player One.

Ending the Game
Players continue rolling the dice and performing the specified actions until they decide that "Foreplay" is over.

MAKE A WISH - The Romantic Version

Number of Couples 1

Supplies
- One sheet of paper (for keeping score)
- One strip of paper per player
- One pen or pencil per player

Setup
Each player writes down a wish to be carried out if he or she wins the game. The wish should be something that the couple can enjoy together. An example of such a wish is "We'll cover each other with caramel and make love on the back porch." Players should not share their wishes with each other until the end of the game.

Play
Player One begins by asking Player Two a trivia question about herself. The question should be true/false or multiple choice (with only two options). It should also be about one of her likes, her past, or her aspirations. An example is "What do I find more relaxing: (a) a hot bath or (b) watching television?" Player Two then attempts to guess the answer. If Player Two guesses correctly, he scores a point. If Player Two is incorrect, he scores zero points.

Next, Player Two poses the same type of question to Player
One. Player One guesses and scores a point if she is correct.
Players continue asking each other questions until one of them
has scored ten points.

Ending the Game
The first player to score ten points wins the game. At this
point the runner-up should share his wish, but it should not be
carried out. The winner then shares her wish, and the couple
carries it out.

MAKE A WISH SAMPLE QUESTIONS

1. Where would I rather make love?
   a) a freshly plowed field
   b) a secluded rooftop
2. True or False. I enjoy the time I spend with your family.
3. True or False. I have been completely happy with our love life lately.
4. If I were stranded on a deserted island, with whom would I rather be stranded?
   a) my boss
   b) your first girlfriend/boyfriend
5. What do I find to be more romantic?
   a) a moonlit stroll
   b) breakfast in bed
6. True or False. The idea of being lost in the wilderness frightens the hell out of me.
7. True or False. I have never engaged in phone sex.
8. What would I rather have as a pet?
   a) a chimpanzee
   b) a boa constrictor
9. True or False. My greatest asset is my sense of humor.
10. True or False. When I retire, I would like to consider moving to Arizona or Florida.
11. What do I dream about more?
    a) high school
    b) sex
12. True or False. I would rather start making love to you right now than continue playing this game.

13. True or False. I have kept a journal (or diary) at some point during my life.

14. What would I rather receive as a gift from you?

    a) a back massage

    b) a dozen carnations

15. True or False. I would take a job emptying portable restrooms if I were offered double my current salary.

16. True or False. At some point during my education, I have received straight As.

17. What prop would I rather use while making love?

    a) handcuffs

    b) whipped cream

18. True or False. I think I was cool in high school.

19. True or False. I am an adventurous person.

20. What would I rather win?

    a) a Nobel prize

    b) first place in a beauty pageant

21. True or False. I have never fallen asleep while driving.

22. True or False. I enjoy watching cartoons, but only once in a while.

23. True or False. I would like to audition for a game show.

24. True or False. I usually remember my dreams.

25. True or False. I have seriously considered writing a book.

26. What vacation spot would I rather visit?

    a) Hawaii

    b) Egypt

27. True or False. I think puppet shows are cute.

28. True or False. I was the president of at least one organization in high school.

29. What super power would I rather possess?

    a) super-human strength

    b) the ability to fly

30. True or False. I have appeared on television.

MAKE A WISH - The Mean Version

Number of Couples 1

Supplies
- One sheet of paper (for keeping score)
- One strip of paper per player
- One pen or pencil per player

Setup
Each player writes down a chore to be carried out by the other player. The chore should be an unpleasant activity that either or both players want done. An example of such a chore is "Scrub the grout between the bathroom floor tiles." Players should not share their chores with each other until the end of the game.

Play
Player One begins by asking Player Two a trivia question about himself. The question should be true/false or multiple choice (with only two options). It should also be about one of his dislikes, his recent upsets, or his negative opinions. An example is, "What do I find more annoying: (a) screaming kids or (b) collect call commercials?" Player Two then attempts to guess the answer. If Player Two guesses correctly, she scores a point. If Player Two is incorrect, she scores zero points.

Next, Player Two poses the same type of question to Player One. Player One guesses and scores a point if he is correct. Players continue asking each other questions until one of them has scored ten points.

Ending the Game

The first player to score ten points wins the game. At this point the runner-up should share her chore, but it should not be carried out by her partner. The winner then shares his chore, and relaxes as he watches his partner carry it out.

MAKE A WISH SAMPLE QUESTIONS (Mean Version)

1. True or False. I like your taste in clothes.
2. I would be happiest if we spent less time with _____.
   a) your friends
   b) your family
3. True or False. I do not have any deep dark secrets that I have not shared with you.
4. True or False. If I won the lottery, I would give 50% of it to you.
5. Would I rather?
   a) glow in the dark forever
   b) always smell like Swedish meatballs
6. True or False. If an attractive stranger offered me $100 to perform a lap dance, I would do it.
7. True or False. Most of my sex dreams are about you.
8. What area do I feel requires more attention on your part?
   a) your cooking abilities
   b) your cleaning skills
9. True or False. I fully respect your taste in music.
10. True or False. I never drink to escape my problems.
11. I don't spend enough time in the _____.
    a) gym
    b) kitchen
12. True or False. I enjoy watching adult movies once in a while.
13. True or False. You are the naughtiest lover that I have ever had.
14. True or False. If I were offered a free plastic surgery operation of my choice, I would seriously consider it.

15. True of False. I swear sometimes when it is not necessary.

16. What would I rather do?

    a) shave off all my body hair

    b) shave off all your body hair

17. True or False. I could stand to lose a few pounds.

18. True or False. I have never been arrested.

19. True or False. I am sometimes insensitive about your feelings.

20. True or False. I look great in a two-piece swimsuit.

21. If I were a road sign, which one would better suit me?

    a) one way

    b) watch out for falling rocks

22. What would I rather give you right now?

    a) a slap across the face

    b) an enema

23. True or False. At some point in my life, I have had serious problems with acne.

24. After I die, where would I rather be buried?

    a) under the swing set at my favorite childhood playground

    b) at the base of the nearest mountain

25. True or False. I have never had sexual relations with someone who is married to another person.

26. True or False. I think I have beautiful hair.

27. What needs to be updated more?

    a) my wardrobe

    b) my hairstyle

28. True or False. Your friends think you made an excellent choice when you decided to start dating me.

29. I have fewer hopes of ever becoming a _____.

    a) stand-up comic

    b) chef

30. True or False. I have never been accused of being an alcoholic.

SEDUCTION

Number of Couples 1

Supplies
- A hat (or similar container)
- Eight strips of paper
- An erasable ink pen (or chalk)
- A damp cloth

Setup

The seducer writes the following actions individually on eight strips of paper:

- Caress
- Kiss
- Lick
- Massage
- Nibble
- Stroke
- Suck
- Tickle

The seducer folds the strips of paper in half and places them inside the hat. He then has his partner undress completely. He takes the erasable ink pen and writes the numbers one through eight on his partner.

Starting at one, the following is the list of body parts that should be labeled:

1. Cheek
2. Ears
3. Lips (label should be placed close by)
4. Neck
5. Chest
6. Stomach
7. Inner thighs
8. Genitals (label should be placed close by)

Play

The seducer selects an entry from the hat and performs the action listed on the slip of paper. Since this is the first draw, he performs the action on the cheek of his partner. (He may wish to use the damp cloth to remove the ink first). His performance should last two to five minutes.

Next he draws the second entry, and performs the action on his partner's ears (the body part labeled with the '2'). He continues drawing entries and performing actions until all eight body parts have received their appropriate attention.

Variation

A couple could easily adjust the rules of this game to allow for reciprocation. In this version, there would be two sets of eight actions, two hats, and both partners would have their body parts labeled. Then partners would take turns drawing actions and performing them on each other.

WARNING!

Do not play the PHYSICAL CONTACT games with players that have any kind of communicable illness or disease. Also, you may wish to exclude players with poor hygiene (if you believe that they could be hosting any kind of virus or germ that you do not wish to share).

PHYSICAL

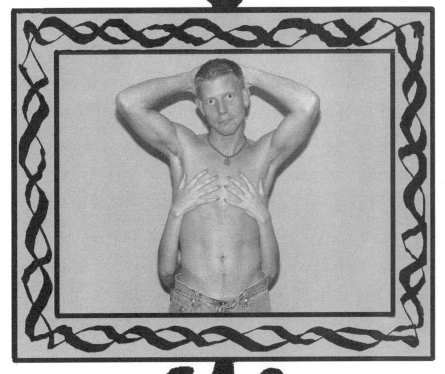

CONTACT

I DON'T THINK SO!

Number of Players 4+

These instructions should not be shared with the person who volunteers to be in the center of the circle, because the object of the game is for that person to figure out the game's secret.

Setup

One player, who is not familiar with this game, volunteers to be in the center and leaves the room. After she (Player One) departs, the other players sit in a circle and the host describes the secret of the game to them.

Play

Player One enters into the center of the circle and begins asking the other players personal questions. The secret of the game is that each player is answering as if he or she is another person in the circle. After Player One asks Player Two a question, Player Two selects another person in the circle (Player Three) and answers the question as if he were her. Then he walks to her, kisses her cheek, and returns to his seat.

If Player Two has answered the question incorrectly for Player Three, she says, "I don't think so!" If Player Two has answered appropriately, Player Three does not say anything after the kiss. Player One continues by asking another personal question of any one of the other players.

There are a few rules that Player One must follow when querying the other players:

- No asking about the significance of the phrase "I don't think so!"
- No asking about the reason why players are kissing each others' cheeks.
- No asking for clues or hints about the secret of the game.
- If Player One wishes to make a guess about the secret of the game, it must be in the form of a yes/no question. (For example, "Is the secret that players are answering how they would have answered five years ago?")

If Player One violates a rule, there is no penalty, but she must ask a new question. Also, Player One may attempt to guess the secret of the game at any time. The other players should not let Player One know if her guess is close to the truth. For example, if she asks whether people are answering as if they are players on the opposite side of the circle, she should simply be told that she has not guessed the secret.

Ending the Game
If and when Player One identifies the secret, she wins the game.

Variation

If Player One is unable to guess the secret in a reasonable amount of time, the group may appoint an assistant. The assistant (who knows the secret) joins Player One in the center of the circle and takes over as the one who asks the questions. The assistant should ask questions that entertain the group, as well as ones that provide clues to Player One about the game's secret.

HUMAN LIMBO

Number of Players 4+

Setup

The player with the longest legs begins the first round of the game by standing bowlegged in the middle of the playing area (and thus becomes the limbo person for the round). The rest of the players line up in front of the limbo person.

Play

Players each take a turn at attempting to limbo between the limbo person's legs. They are allowed to touch the limbo person, but not with their hands. If a player touches him with her hands, she must exit from the game. Also, a player who touches the ground with either her knees or bottom should be eliminated.

The second round begins after each player has made an attempt at limboing under the player with the longest legs. The remaining player with the second longest legs stands bowlegged in the middle of the playing area. The other remaining players, including the limbo person from the previous round, then attempt to limbo between the new limbo person's legs. The remaining player with the next shortest legs becomes the limbo person for the next round.

Ending the Game

Play continues until one of the following occurs:

- Players have limboed under the player with the shortest legs.
- The only player remaining in the game is the limbo person.

Each player remaining in the game (when either point is reached) is considered a winner of the game.

NAUGHTINESS

Number of Players 4+

Supplies
- A hat (or similar container)
- Five strips of paper per player
- One pen or pencil per player

Setup
Each player thinks of five "naughty acts" and writes them
individually on five strips of paper. Naughty acts are
essentially dares that any player in the group could be capable
of carrying out. Examples of naughty acts include "Pull down
your pants." and "Make out with the player to your right."
Naughty acts can be general (like the previous examples) or
they can be tailored to pick on an individual. An example of
the latter is "Make out with Claudia." Players should write
their initials in a corner of each entry they submit. Entries
should be folded and placed into the hat.

Play
Player One begins by selecting an entry from the hat. She then
carries out the action listed or drops out of the game. If she
drops out of the game, the author must then carry out the action
listed. If he does not wish to do so, he must also drop out of
the game. Once the action is carried out (or if Player One and
the author of the entry drop out), the action is discarded. Also,
the subject of the dare has the option to drop out of the game.

For example, if the naughty act is "Make out with Claudia," Claudia may refuse to participate and drop out of the game. If the subject drops out (or is no longer a player of the game), the author of the entry should appoint another player to be the new subject.

Next, Player Two draws an entry and carries out the action (or drops out). Play continues until all players have drawn an action. Then Player One starts the next round by drawing another entry.

At any point, a player may contest another player's performance in carrying out an action. If at least half of the group agrees that the player's performance was unsatisfactory, the player must make a second attempt or drop out of the game.

Players continue acting out entries until only one player remains. If the supply of entries has been depleted, then the remaining players each submit five more entries and continue playing.

Ending the Game
The last person remaining in the game is the winner. The host should award a prize to this person.

SEDUCE THE PIG

Number of Players 3+

These instructions are to be read only by the host, since the object of the game is to trick participants into performing embarrassing acts.

Setup

Players sit in a circle. The host explains to the group that he has an imaginary pig in his hands that he will soon be passing around. He informs the group that this pig is a very beautiful pig; in fact, it is the most sexually enticing creature that they have ever laid their eyes on. He instructs the group that, as the pig is passed around, each player should explain what they would do to seduce this beautiful creature.

Play

The host begins the game by announcing what he will do to seduce the pig (e.g., kiss it passionately on the neck). He then carries out the seduction on the imaginary pig (e.g., by passionately kissing its imaginary neck). He then passes the imaginary pig to the player on his left. Participants are not allowed to name an act of seduction that has already been selected by another player. Players continue selecting different acts and carrying them out on the imaginary pig, until the pig is returned to the host. The host then announces the instructions for the second round of the game. Each player now has to perform his or her previously stated act of seduction on the player to his or her left. The host begins the second round by performing the act he selected on the player to his left. This player then performs her seduction act on the player to her left. The game continues in this manner until the host receives the seduction act from the player on his right.

Ending the Game

Everyone wins this game (except the player sitting next to the sadist).

STATUES

Number of Players 6+

These instructions are to be read only by the host, since the object of the game is to trick participants into an uncomfortable position.

Play

The host selects two volunteers and asks the rest of the players to leave the room. She should direct them to a room (or other location) where they will not be able to hear what is said in the playing area. Once all other players are out of the room, the host explains to the two volunteers that they are statues. As statues, they are portraying a romantic scene and should pose accordingly. They should hold the pose until they are instructed to do otherwise.

The host then pulls someone out of the group that was previously asked to leave the room. The person is escorted to the statue and informed that he is a sculptor and his job is to make the statue slightly more risque by adjusting the pose of one of the statue participants. Once his adjustment is complete, the host informs him that he must now replace the person whose pose he adjusted. He must assume the same position of the person he replaces.

The host leads the next person into the room and repeats the instructions to the new sculptor. The sculptor adjusts one of the statue participants, then assumes her position in the statue. This process is repeated for each of the remaining players that are watching in the other room.

Winning the Game

The game ends after the last sculptor has assumed his position in the sculpture. There are no winners to this game.

FIRST DATE

Number of Players 6+

Supplies
- A hat (or similar container)
- A variety of acting props (e.g., chairs, wine glasses, and whipped cream)
- Scissors

Setup

In preparation for this game, the host should photocopy the list of body parts that follows this game (or develop a similar list). She should then separate the words by cutting along the lines. The host folds the strips of paper and places the entries in a hat.

The host (with assistance from the other party guests) appoints two people to be the actors in this game. The two actors will be going on their "first date," so the host may want to use this opportunity to get two people together that she always thought would make a good match. The two actors stand at the front of the room. The other players sit at least a few feet away from them in order to give them a stage area for their skit. They should try to sit in a circle.

Play

One of the other guests volunteers to be the first storyteller. He should start by explaining where the two actors are (for example, Actor One has just picked Actor Two up from her house, and is driving them to a restaurant). The actors then arrange themselves in the setting that the storyteller describes. If appropriate, they should use the props provided.

The storyteller then begins telling the story of the two actors' first date and the actors act out whatever the storyteller describes (but they only mouth words if the storyteller has them speak). Within a few sentences, the storyteller should have one of the actors make some kind of move on the other. The storyteller says something like, "Sally then grabbed onto David's <blank> with one quick movement." The host then fills in the blank by selecting one of the strips of paper from the hat and the actors act out the continuation of the story appropriately. The storyteller should use a <blank> only as a replacement for a part of the body. Also, selected strips of paper should be discarded after they are used.

The storytelling responsibility now switches to the next person in the circle. The replacement storyteller must pick up the story where the previous one left off.

Ending the Game

The story continues until after the last strip of paper is selected. At this point, the storyteller is allowed only a few sentences to wrap up the story. If the actors end up hooking up after the game ends, then they can be considered winners of the game.

FIRST DATE GAME PIECES

LIPS	EYELID
PINKY	BIG TOE
INNER THIGH	RIGHT BUTTOCK
GENITAL	BELLY BUTTON
NOSE	HIP
NECK	TONGUE
HAIR	ARMPIT
ANKLE	WRIST
KNEECAP	NIPPLE
EYEBROW	CHEEK
FOREHEAD	LEFT HAND
ANAL CAVITY	EARLOBE

FRUIT BOWL RACES

Number of Players 2

Supplies
- Four bowls of equal size
- Several pieces of fruit

Setup
The host places four bowls on the floor. The first two bowls should be on one side of the room, a couple feet apart from each other. The other two bowls are placed straight across from the first two bowls, on the other side of the room. The host then fills the first two bowls with several pieces of fruit. The types of fruit and the number of pieces should be the same for both bowls.

The host selects two volunteers (before explaining the rules). Each player stands next to a fruit bowl and the audience clears a path between them and the bowls on the opposite side of the room.

Play
After the host says "go," the two players race to transfer fruit from their bowls on one side of the room, to their bowls on the other side. Each player should only select fruit from his assigned bowl and deposit it in the bowl directly across from it.

The players are not allowed to

- Touch the fruit with their hands or mouths.
- Touch the floor with their hands.
- Deposit fruit anywhere other than their appropriate bowls.
- Carry more than one piece of fruit at a time.
- Lift either of their bowls off the floor.
- Touch the other player.

The audience members should inform the host if they notice a contestant violating one of the rules. After a contestant violates a rule, the host should take the fruit that she is currently carrying and place it back into her starting bowl. If she violates a rule but does not have fruit that she is currently transporting, the host should take a piece of fruit from the finishing bowl and place it into her starting bowl.

At any point during the game, contestants may remove, unfasten, or loosen articles of clothing. They can use their hands for this, but clothing cannot be taken off until after the host has started the contest.

Ending the Game
The first player to successfully deposit all her fruit into the second bowl wins the game. The host should award a prize to this player.

WARNING!

It is recommended that the RISQUÉ DRINKING games be played with nonalcoholic beverages. If players do decide to play these games with alcohol, they should carefully determine how many drinks they can safely consume before starting each game.

IMPORTANT: A player should ignore a drink assignment and quit a game if taking the drink causes the player to exceed his or her set limit.

DON'T DRINK AND DRIVE. Do not play these games with alcohol if you will be driving afterwards.

The RISQUÉ DRINKING games also involve physical contact with other players. Do not play these games with players that have any kind of communicable illness or disease. Also, you may wish to exclude players with poor hygiene (if you believe that they could be hosting any kind of virus or germ that you do not wish to share).

DRINKING METER (1 can of beer = 10 drinks)

NAME THAT TRAMP

Number of Players 4+

Supplies
- A hat (or similar container)
- Five strips of paper per player
- Several pens or pencils
- A full beverage per player

Setup
One of the players, typically the host of the party, emcees the game. All players (except the emcee) write down the full names of five people they have slept with. The entries should be written individually on five strips of paper. If a player has not had five sex partners, she can supplement her entries by adding people she has only made out with. In this instance, she should write down "MO" in parentheses after the person's name. Players should also include their names (or initials) on each entry they submit. Completed entries should be folded and placed in the hat. After everyone has submitted their entries, the emcee collects them and sits at the front of the room.

Play
The emcee draws a name out of the hat and reads it to the group. If a player thinks that he knows the author of the entry, he should yell out her name. He is allowed only one guess

though. If he is incorrect, he has to take a drink. Other players continue wagering guesses (and drinking if they are incorrect) until someone guesses correctly. This person gets to assign three drinks to other players in the room. She can assign all three drinks to the same person, or she may split them up and assign them to two or three players. If all players are disqualified from wagering a second guess before the player's name is revealed, the emcee should discard the entry without revealing who wrote it. The emcee continues presenting the entries until all of the entries have been guessed or discarded.

Ending the Game

The game ends after the emcee has presented all of the entries. The person who has made the most correct guesses is the winner of the game.

ROLL OFF ALL YOUR CLOTHES?

Number of Players 3+

Supplies
- Two dice
- A full beverage per player

Setup
Players seat themselves in a circle or around a table.

Play
Players take turns rolling both dice and carrying out specific actions based on the numbers rolled. When a player rolls one of the numbers listed below, she must take the appropriate action. The rolls and corresponding actions are as follows:

      4 - Put on an article of clothing.
      5 - Take a drink.
      7 - Remove an article of clothing.
      9 - Take a drink.
      10 - Put on an article of clothing.
      11 - Remove an article of clothing.
   Doubles - Make a rule.

After a player removes an article of clothing, she places it in the center of the table. She may block the roll (by taking five drinks) if she wishes not to remove clothing. A player can only put on an article of clothing if there is one in the center of the table that he has not yet worn during the course of the game. If a player rolls doubles, she may devise a rule that pertains to how the game is played. Examples of rules are "Take a drink if you say a word that starts with the letter 'D'." and "Remove an article of clothing if you speak a sentence with more than four words." Rules can be used against other rules. For example, the rule could state that the last two rules given by other players are no longer applicable.

A player continues rolling until at least one of her dice is a six, then she passes the dice to the next player.

Ending the Game
A player is eliminated from the game when he is no longer wearing any clothing. A player can also be eliminated if he wishes to excuse himself from the game. The last player remaining in the game is the winner

BODY SHOT RACES

Number of Players 10

Supplies
- Two shot glasses
- Two bottles of tequila (or other liquor/beverage)
- Eight lime wedges
- Two salt shakers

Setup
Players divide themselves into two teams of five. One player on each team volunteers to be the "body" for the race. The two bodies remove their shirts and sit on the floor (with at least two to three feet of space between them). The host may want to place a tarp or blanket underneath them, if she is worried about tequila being spilled on the floor (or the game should be played outdoors). The bodies should sit with their legs stretched out and they should lean back so their backs are close to forming 45-degree angles from the floor.

The remaining four players (on each team) line up in front of their team's body. The last person in line will assist with the first shot, so he should crouch next to his team's body. Each assistant collects one shot glass, one bottle of tequila, four lime wedges, and one salt shaker.

Play

One of the players says "go," and the first players in line approach the bodies. The assistants place salt beneath the bodies' navels and place the lime wedges at the edge of the bodies' mouths (with the rinds facing inward). The assistants pour full shots of tequila into their shot glasses and move so that they are behind their team's bodies. The two shot-takers then lick the salt off the bodies, and the assistants pour the shots down the torsos of the bodies. The shots should be poured at the top of the chest and should be aimed so that they pour towards the bodies' navels. The shot-takers catch the shots in their mouths at the bodies' navels, then they bite the lime wedges out of the bodies' mouths. If a shot-taker does not drink at least half of the poured shot, she must take a second body shot.

After the shot is completed, the assistant returns to the end of the line, the previous shot-taker becomes the new assistant, and the next person in line becomes the next shot-taker. Play continues until all four players successfully consume a body shot.

Ending the Game

The team that completes all four body shots first wins the game. They are then able to assign a five-shot penalty. The team decides as a group who on their opposing team will take the penalty. They can distribute the penalty equally by requiring each player to take one, or they can assign more than one to some players and zero to others.

WARNING!

It is recommended that the DRINKING games be played with nonalcoholic beverages. If players do decide to play these games with alcohol, they should carefully determine how many drinks they can safely consume before starting each game.

IMPORTANT: A player should ignore a drink assignment and quit a game if taking the drink causes the player to exceed his or her set limit.

DON'T DRINK AND DRIVE. Do not play these games with alcohol if you will be driving afterwards.

TRADITIONAL

DRINKING

DRINKING METER (1 can of beer = 10 drinks)

REMOTE CONTROL

Number of Players 2+

Supplies

- A television with remote control
- A pair of scissors
- A hat (or similar container)
- A one minute hourglass timer (or stopwatch)
- A full beverage per player

Setup

In preparation for this game, the host should photocopy the list of items that follows these instructions (or develop a similar list). She should separate the list of items by cutting along the lines. Completed entries should be folded and placed in a hat.

Play

Players take turns selecting items from the hat and attempting to locate them by clicking through the channels. The first volunteer begins the game by selecting an item from the hat. She reads the entry to the group, flips over the timer, and begins clicking through the available television channels. If she runs out of time before finding her item, she must take three drinks. If she locates her item within the allotted minute, she informs the group of her find. Then everyone in the group must take a drink. Members of the group can protest if they do not think her find legitimately matches the item she selected.

If more than half the group protests, her find is invalid and she must continue flipping through the channels (unless her time has already run out).

The first volunteer then discards her strip of paper. The next volunteer draws an item and takes a turn at locating it with the remote control. Players continue volunteering to take turns, thereby establishing a turn order. Players should try to maintain the turn order, but new guests may jump in at any time.

Ending the Game
Play should continue until all strips of paper have been used. There are no winners to this game.

REMOTE CONTROL GAME PIECES

A ROMANTIC SCENE	SOMETHING UNETHICAL
A PUFFY WHITE CLOUD	ALCOHOL/DRUG USE
A POLITICAL FIGURE	SOMEONE YELLING
A GAY CHARACTER OR ACTOR	AN OVER-USED AD ICON OR SLOGAN
A WASHED-UP CHILD ACTOR	GAUDY JEWELRY
VILLAINOUS BEHAVIOR	A CAFFEINATED BEVERAGE
A DAIRY PRODUCT	A FARM ANIMAL
A NERD	ANY FORM OF LITTER OR POLLUTION
BELL-BOTTOM PANTS	A CIGARETTE
AN ABSORBENT PRODUCT	A HIGHLY FLAMMABLE MATERIAL
RUNNING WATER	AN EMMY AWARD WINNER
LIVE COVERAGE	BIG HAIR
AN INFOMERCIAL OR TELETHON	SOMEONE LYING IN A HOSPITAL BED
A MELODRAMATIC MOMENT (NOT ON LIFETIME)	CARTOON CHARACTERS CHASING EACH OTHER
A REDHEAD	A MAN WITH HIS SHIRT OFF
A BABY CRYING	A TURBAN

SHOT GLASS RACES

Number of Players 8

Supplies
- Two quarters
- Two shot glasses
- One beer mug
- A full pitcher of beer

Setup
Players divide themselves into two teams of four. The teams
line up on opposite sides of a table.

Each team designates an anchor. The anchors should be
opposite each other at one end of the table. The anchors will
be the last members of their teams to attempt to bounce
quarters into their teams' shot glasses. The players at the other
end of the table will start the game. They each need a quarter
and a shot glass.

Play
One of the players says "go" and the first two players attempt
to bounce their quarters into their teams' shot glasses. Each
player must bounce the quarter as many times as it takes until
the quarter lands into the shot glass. After a successful bounce,
the player passes the shot glass and quarter to the second player

of the team. The second player then attempts to bounce the quarter into the shot glass. After she is successful, she passes the shot glass and quarter to the third player. After the third player is successful, she passes the shot glass and quarter to the anchor.

The team whose anchor lands the quarter into the shot glass before the other anchor, wins the round for the team. The losing team then has to take the penalty drinks. The losing team fills up the beer mug and then the first player begins drinking from it. He can drink as little or as much beer as he chooses. After he finishes, he passes the mug to the second player. She drinks what she wants, then passes it to the third player. After the third player drinks, the mug is passed to the anchor. The anchor must finish the beer.

Before the next round begins, the anchors of each team are permitted to designate other team members to be the new anchors. If a new anchor is appointed, the old and new anchors swap seats (or positions) at the table.

Ending the Game
Players continue playing rounds until the pitcher is empty. The team that has drunk the least number of times can be considering the winning team of the game.

Tips on Bouncing the Quarter

Hold the quarter between your thumb and pointer finger. It should be horizontal and about six inches above the table. Use a quick jerking motion when you throw it down to the table. The height of the bounce will vary depending on the surface of the table (the quarter should not bounce more than a couple of inches above the shot glass).

WHO IS THE PUSSY?

Number of Players 8+

Supplies
- A deck of regular playing cards
- A full beverage per player

Setup
One of the players, typically the host of the party, starts the game as the conductor. In preparation for this game, she needs to select one red card and several black cards from a deck of playing cards. The number of black cards she pulls will vary (she should have one less black card than the total number of players).

Play
The conductor shuffles the cards and deals them out so that each player has one card. Players view their cards, but should not let anyone else see what they were dealt. The person with the red card is the "pussy." Everyone else is a "mutt."

After all players have viewed their cards, the conductor begins waving his hands. As he moves his hands back and forth, he says, "One, two, three." Next he says "now" and points to the group. In normal speaking voices, the mutts say "woof" and the pussy says "rowr."

The conductor selects any one of the players and asks him, "Who is the pussy?" He then wagers a guess. If he is correct, he becomes the conductor for the next round. If he is incorrect, he takes a drink. Then the conductor selects another player and asks her, "Who is the pussy?"

The conductor continues asking players, "Who is the pussy?" until someone guesses correctly. If she asks the pussy, the pussy can either lie and take a drink or can reveal that she is the pussy. If she reveals her identity, she becomes the conductor for the next round.

Ending the Game
Play should continue until players feel that they have reached a natural ending point.

PERSONAL TRIVIA

Number of Players 8+

Supplies

- One hat (or similar container) per team
- One strip of paper per player
- Several pens or pencils
- A full beverage per player

Setup

One of the players, typically the host of the party, emcees the game. Players divide themselves into two teams of four or more players. The teams do not have to have the same number of players, but the group should try to split as evenly as possible.

Each player writes a true experience on a piece of paper. Players should choose personal experiences that have been kept secret from players on the other team. An example of an entry is "I lost my virginity on the seat of a tractor." Players should not write their names on their entries, and their entries must be actual experiences. Also, players should not show their entries to the players on other teams. Completed entries should be folded and placed in the team's hat. After all players have submitted entries, the teams switch hats.

Play

The emcee draws an entry from Team One's hat. She reads the entry aloud, then Team One attempts to guess which player on Team Two wrote the entry. The team can discuss the entry, but should provide an agreed-upon answer soon after the emcee reads it. The person who Team One guesses then reveals whether or not he wrote the entry. (If he did not write it, the true author should not reveal that she wrote it.) If Team One guesses correctly, every member on Team Two takes a drink. If Team One guesses incorrectly, every member of Team One takes a drink. Next, Team Two draws an entry and attempts to guess which player on Team One wrote it.

Ending the Game

Teams continue taking turns drawing entries and wagering guesses until both teams' hats are empty. The team whose members have had to drink the least can be considered winners of this game.

Variation

Players can up the wager for certain types of trivia. For example, entries that are about sexual experiences could be worth two drinks. Then if the team guesses correctly, the other team's members take two drinks each. If they guess incorrectly, each team member takes two drinks.

DIFFICULT QUESTIONS

Number of Players 2+

Supplies
- A full beverage per player

Setup
Players sit in a circle and the group establishes a drink penalty. The group decides how many drinks a player should take if he or she does not wish to answer a question posed by another player. A one drink penalty would be conservative, a two drink penalty is moderate, and three or more might be too extreme for some drinkers.

Play
A volunteer (Player One) asks the group the first "difficult question." The question should be open-ended (i.e., not yes/no or multiple choice). An example of a difficult question is "Who in this room would you most like to seduce?" A list of sample difficult questions follows this game.

Player Two (the player to the left of Player One) either answers the question honestly or takes the drink penalty. The question is then posed to the next player in the circle. Play continues in this manner until all players (besides Player One) have either answered the question honestly or taken the drink penalty.

Player Two poses a second difficult question to the group, the player on her left poses a third question, and so on.

A player is allowed to challenge another if she feels that he has not answered a question honestly. She then has to explain why she is challenging the answer, and the player is allowed to respond to the accusation. If a majority of the group feels that the player is indeed lying, he has to take double the drink penalty. If the majority believes the player is telling the truth, the person who challenged him has to take double the drink penalty.

Ending the Game

Play should continue until players feel that they have reached a natural ending point. There are no winners to this game.

SAMPLE DIFFICULT QUESTIONS

1. What is the sleaziest thing that you have ever done?
2. What is the most illegal thing that you have ever done?
3. With which two people in this room would you most want to have a threesome?
4. If you had to break one of the other players' arms, whom would you choose? (The person asking the question should be excluded from the possible choices.)
5. What is your favorite thing to do in bed?
6. When was the last time someone else heard you fart?
7. Of the people who have appeared in your sex dreams, whom are you most ashamed to name?
8. If you had to have sexual relations with an animal, what type of animal would you choose?
9. Excluding yourself, who in the room do you imagine looks the best naked?
10. If you were stranded on a deserted island, which other player would you most prefer to have stranded with you?
11. When was the last time that you masturbated?
12. Who in the room have you heard the worst gossip about?
13. Do you prefer to spank others, or would you rather be spanked?
14. Which other player would you least like to have locked in a closet with you?
15. How much money would someone have to pay you for you to ostracize yourself completely from the person sitting to your left?